CAREERS IN

TOUR OPERATION

TRAVEL MARKETING

MOST PEOPLE WANT SOME EXCITEMENT in their lives. Tour operators provide excitement in doses small enough to squeeze into real life and big enough to make memories to last a lifetime. There are tour operators to cater to every fascination, from classic adventures like safaris and exotic camping trips, to simpler excursions like neighborhood tours and organized pub crawls. The market for tours is endless, and so are the opportunities for employment and entrepreneurship.

According to the United States Tour Operators Association, an industry trade group, Americans spend about $15 billion every year on organized tours and vacation packages. A growing number of Americans have discretionary income and like to use it to do things that are out of the ordinary. Most people are also a little leery of diving into complicated travel planning, especially when the travel is to far-flung places or involves some element of risk. Then there is the language barrier. How many Americans can negotiate lodging arrangements in, say, Tajikistan? That is where tour operators come in. They take the hassle, confusion, and risk out of travel planning.

You are looking into this profession at an opportune time. Americans are spending more on travel than ever before. Relatively inexpensive tours and vacation packages become more popular every year as more people decide to leave the detailed planning to somebody with knowledge and expertise. High-end tours also seem to know no bounds. The priciest tours can top $10,000 per day and take travelers to places they could never get to on their own.

Would you like to be the one designing these experiences and making all the arrangements for a perfect journey?

WHAT YOU CAN DO NOW

THERE ARE PLENTY OF WAYS TO GET some experience in tour operation before you commit to the career path. Scrounge the websites of tour operators to see what they offer. It is really easy to spend a few hours perusing the websites of tour operators. Tour operators offer dreams.

Want to knock something off your travel bucket list? Chances are there is a tour operator out there that can make your wish come true. You will be amazed at the touring opportunities you find on the web. You may also be amazed at what some tours cost. You may not be able to afford them, but you could be a part of providing them. Most people would love to be paid to do something they would happily do for free.

The top-priced tours are amazing and amazingly expensive. You may also be surprised to find that many tours are very reasonably priced and close to home. You can start with something very simple, like a free tour of a historic home in your city. Such tours are often provided by historical societies, and the guides tend to be volunteers, called docents. This is touring in its simplest form, and it is a good place to start. If you live in a major metropolitan area, there are undoubtedly many tours to choose from. Most New York natives, for example, have never been to the Statue of Liberty. Most Chicagoans have never taken any of the tours offered by the Chicago Architecture Foundation.

If you like those historical society tours you go on, become a volunteer and lead tours yourself. You will learn about basics like customer service and public speaking. You will also learn about scheduling and maybe even bookkeeping and marketing. You can also broaden your horizons by starting your own tour business. Is there something near you that you think is interesting enough to warrant a tour? Do you live near a historic neighborhood? Come up with a tour and see how many people you can attract.

HISTORY OF THE CAREER

TOURISM HAS A LONGER HISTORY than you might think. Most people did not get to travel much until fairly recently, but the wealthy have been venturing forth for centuries. Intrepid and imaginative providers have been there to serve them every step of the way.

It could be argued that the earliest humans were also the earliest tourists. Unable to grow their own food, they had no choice but to roam far and wide in search of animals to hunt and wild fruit and vegetables to harvest. These nomads traveled to survive and it would be a stretch to say that they enjoyed it. Ironically, many modern-day business travelers feel the same way today.

In the distant past, the only people who traveled for pleasure were royalty and explorers looking for adventure. Royalty traveled with enormous retinues of servants, guides, translators, bodyguards, cooks and other assistants who made their trips easier and more enjoyable. Explorers, on the other hand, often traveled alone or in small groups and were self-sufficient. Explorers often worked for kings and queens and helped their royal patrons to expand their realms. Kings and queens built roads to assist commerce and to lay claim to additional territory. Entrepreneurs helped out by building inns and taverns along the way to service travelers passing through.

Modern tourism began roughly in the mid-1660s with the advent of the Grand Tour, a sumptuous journey often undertaken by wealthy young men as part of their education. The Grand Tour included stops in places associated with the great civilizations of the past, like Rome and Naples. The Grand Tour was especially popular with wealthy Britons, who considered their country to be separate from – and superior to – Europe. Although the Grand Tour was far too expensive for most people, it made an impression upon the upper classes and influenced the more-affordable tourism to come.

Leisure travel for the masses first became feasible in the mid-19th century with the dawn of the Industrial Revolution. Machines gave regular people free time because machines could do more work in less time than people could. The Industrial Revolution helped to create the middle class, the part of the population neither rich nor poor but with enough discretionary income to go on an occasional vacation.

Thomas Cook is generally considered the first businessman to seize upon the idea of organized travel and tourism. He said the idea came to him in 1841 while "walking from Market Harborough to Leicester to attend a meeting of the Temperance Society." The society needed to get about 500 people from Leicester to Loughborough, two English cities about 11 miles apart. Cook made arrangements to take them by train, handling all of the logistics so that the travelers could enjoy the trip. Cook founded a company bearing his name and for the next few decades he offered private tours around the United Kingdom, Europe, Egypt and the United States. He brought his son into the business in 1872, renaming the company Thomas Cook & Son. By 1888 the company had established offices around the world and had sold thousands of individual tours. Today the Thomas Cook Group is one of the largest travel companies in the world, with more than 21,000 employees and offices around the world.

The secret to Cook's success was that he made tourism easy. Making travel arrangements was difficult for most people, especially in the days before telephones or the Internet. Travelers wanting to make reservations at a hotel in a faraway city, for example, had to write a letter to the hotel requesting a reservation and wait for a response. If a room was not available on the requested dates the whole process started over again. It was easy to buy a train ticket to a faraway place but not so easy to figure out how to make a connection after you got there. Thomas Cook did all the work so travelers could enjoy themselves. He also brought down prices because he negotiated preferential rates on behalf of his customers.

Cook's model is essentially unchanged today. Tour companies work with hotels, transportation companies and local experts to devise tours that people will be interested in. They make all the arrangements, iron out the details and bundle the experience into a package with an easy-to-understand itinerary and a single price. Such tours usually cost less than they would if tourists purchased each piece separately, because tour companies can negotiate better deals than individual tourists can.

Some tours are just so difficult to figure out that tourists are happy to pay a premium so they do not have to sort it out themselves. Tours to particularly remote or exotic locations often fall into this category. Almost nobody has the connections, patience or time to figure out a two-week excursion through Africa or Asia. It is much easier to log onto a tour company website and let somebody else do all the work.

The Internet has been a mixed blessing for the travel industry. On the one hand, conventional travel agents have been hard-hit by websites that enable anybody to make their own flight and hotel reservations. On the other hand, making travel so easy has been a huge boon for tour operators because anybody can buy a plane ticket to anywhere. Tour operators sell them a place to stay and something to do when they get there. The Internet has also made it easier than ever to get basic information about faraway places and exciting things to do.

The future of the tour industry looks very bright, indeed. The world gets smaller every day. The cost of travel continues to go down and demand for adventure continues to go up.

WHERE YOU WILL WORK

ONE OF THE ADVANTAGES OF THE TOUR BUSINESS is that you can either live anywhere you want or wherever you find the most interesting. Say, for example, you decide you love the historic neighborhoods in a particular city and want to build a business offering tours of them. Where should you live? Living in one of the historic neighborhoods would be perfect. Tour operators who offer local tours get to live near the places and activities they enjoy most. This adds to their credibility with customers. Everybody prefers a guide with ties to the area, as opposed to an employee from somewhere else. If you can set up shop in an area you know well, that is even better.

Tour operators who offer tours to far-off places can live anywhere they want. Many tour operators sell tours to exotic locations but relatively few actually live there. They maintain extensive local contacts in those areas, and go there often to maintain them and discover new hotels, restaurants, and activities. They may live there for a period of time, but most tour operators catering to Americans are based in the United States. Tour operators typically make arrangements for their customers starting from an airport or hotel near the destination. Guides arrive at the destination a few days in advance to make sure everything is squared away and ready to go, and then meet clients at the airport or hotel where they begin their tour.

You may have to move to start your career, however. As a new careerist, you will probably work for an established company for a few years in order to learn the tour business inside and out. You may choose to work for an established business for your entire career. When you work for somebody else you will have to adhere to their schedule. If you are on a full-time salary, you may be required to lead tours more-or-less constantly, which can be very difficult if you have a family or other responsibilities. If you are paid by the tour you may have more flexibility in your schedule but could earn less money.

DESCRIPTION OF THE WORK

Tour Guides

Tour guides are the most visible part of the tour industry. They are the link between the customers, the tour company, and the places worth touring. If you become a tour guide, you will be forever immortalized in hundreds or even thousands of vacation snaps taken by people who will never forget you.

Titles in this business vary from one employer to the next. For the purposes of this report "tour guides" will be defined as careerists who specialize in leading tours lasting anywhere from an hour to a full day, without travel or the need for overnight accommodations. Careerists who lead longer tours are "tour directors."

Many tour industry professionals get their start as tour guides. This is not surprising, as the tour guides are usually the first contact most people have with professionally led tours. Customers sign up for a tour and meet a guide who tells them something interesting that they did not know before.

Tour guides lead all kinds of tours. Many work on a part-time basis, giving tours of historic neighborhoods near where they live, for example. They may work for somebody else or own a very small company that consists of themselves, a website and a few local connections. Depending upon the content of their tours they may give many tours a day or just one. Often, tour guides establish relationships with larger companies like cruise lines or bus tour companies to provide tours as subcontractors. This is a really good deal for the tour guides, as the larger companies generally handle all of the marketing. They take a percentage of the price, of course, but if a cruise line is sending you hundreds of eager tourists every week, you will be glad to let them take it.

Tour guides come from a very wide variety of backgrounds. Some careerists have local knowledge that they want to share. Others are working toward something else and want an interesting job with flexible hours, like college students. Many are mid-life career-changers who used to do something else and decided to try something new. No matter where they come from, all successful tour guides have a genuine interest in their subject. They may also speak more than one language, depending upon their specialty.

They are also interested in the people they serve. Nowadays it is easy to look up everything you want to know about a place or an activity. Type a few words into a search engine and it is all there, usually with plenty of photos. Tour guides offer a richer, more interesting experience than the Internet provides. Tourists tend to forget the details of a tour pretty quickly but they never forget an inspiring guide.

Tour Directors

Tour directors do all the same things tour guides do, and much more. Whereas tour guides get to start over every few hours and then go home at night, tour directors are on the job for days or weeks at a time and have to juggle complex logistics as they go. Many tour directors start out as tour guides and work their way up to longer tours.

Tour directors lead tour groups for long tours that involve travel and overnight accommodation. This can get very complicated and is definitely not a job for amateurs. Tour directors live alongside the people they lead, staying in the same hotels, eating in the same restaurants and dealing with the same issues as they come up. Tour directors working overseas need to be fluent in local languages in order to be able to take care of business while on tour.

Tour directors typically serve as tour guides during their tours, but not all the time. A tour director on a week-long bus tour, for example, will probably give tours of several locations on the tour, as well as provide narration while onboard the bus. However, the director will hand the group off to specialized tour guides from time to time. This usually happens when the tour group arrives at a destination that has its own tour guide program, like a museum or historic site. In these instances, it is the tour director's responsibility to make sure the group arrives on time and meets the proper guide for the tour. Once the tourists have been handed off to the local guide, the director – who has probably been on the tour numerous times – can work on other arrangements or take a break.

Confirming hotel and restaurant reservations requires constant attention. And checking on the weather. And finding alternatives in the event a destination is unexpectedly closed. Tour directors are logisticians as much as guides. Their knowledge of the Eiffel Tower, for example, is not worth much if the hotel reservations get botched up and the group has to stay far away, forcing the director to find something else interesting to do. Tour directors always have to be one step ahead of their itinerary.

This is not an easy job. A tour group of 30 people will almost always include a few troublesome personalities who do not get along, a handful of high-maintenance types who are never happy, and even a few ultra-enthusiastic fans who want to monopolize the tour director's time with non-stop questions. Add to this the need to keep to a strict schedule of hotel and restaurant reservations, show up on time to take guided tours, and be ready to improvise if something goes wrong and you have a very challenging job.

Adventure Guides and Directors

  Adventure guides and directors do the same thing as regular tour guides and directors but within the adventure segment of the industry. Broadly defined, tour adventures consist of an exotic locale and/or a challenging physical activity. Adventures may last a few hours, days or weeks. Adventures also require more than just local knowledge and logistical skill. Adventure careerists need something else. What that is varies. African Safari directors, for example, need to be willing and able to live in tents for long periods of time and to deal with the challenges they will face while on safari, from tropical diseases, to wild animal attacks, to unexpected political turmoil. This requires in-depth local knowledge, language ability and fearless tenacity to overcome the odds. Not all tours are about leisurely moving from one hotel to the next while checking out a few sights in-between.

There are other types of adventures, too. The tour director on a whitewater rafting expedition must be an excellent athlete, able to safely navigate a raft through potentially treacherous waterways. This kind of tour director needs in-depth knowledge and ability in a particular activity. This skill will be necessary to teach the tourists how to perform the activity safely and to have fun. If you want to lead cycling tours around French wine country, for example, riding a bike 100 miles a day is something you should do effortlessly.

All tour guides and tour directors need to keep safety in mind at all times. Leading groups can be challenging under the best of circumstances, as people often wander off or get lost. Adventure guides and directors need to be prepared for anything and everything. Consider advanced first aid training to be mandatory for these careers.

Tour Consultant/Itinerary Specialist

Tour consultants and itinerary specialists – the titles are commonly used to describe essentially similar jobs – are the experts who spend most of their time in the headquarters office supporting the guides and directors in the field. Itinerary specialists are often former tour directors who want to spend more time at home and less on the road. Itinerary specialists usually work behind the scenes to find hotels, restaurants, and things to do, and then devise itineraries around them. They tend to be experts in certain regions or activities, who have been in the tour business for a long time.

Itinerary specialists generally devise itineraries in response to market demand. If customers are clamoring for more ways to take in the wonders of Argentina, say, intrepid itinerary specialists come up with new tours to meet the demand. They may hit the road for a few weeks to check out the options in-person and make local connections. They negotiate deals and lay the groundwork for the tours to come. When they have a new itinerary all figured out they advertise it and hand it off to tour directors.

Itinerary specialists are also the critical points of contact for tour directors working in the field. Tour directors often need help from their home office, especially when it comes to unexpected diversions or expenses. Itinerary specialists often have access to additional resources not available to tour directors on the road. They can also approve or disapprove of options being considered by the tour director.

Entrepreneurs/Business Owner

The tour industry is a very entrepreneurial business. Click on the About Us section on tour company websites and you will find many inspirational stories about the founders, many of whom started their companies almost on a whim and never looked back. Globe-straddling tour companies with offices around the world may not look like scrappy start-ups any more but you may be surprised at how many began as nothing more than a good idea and a ton of ambition and energy.

STORIES OF TOUR INDUSTRY PROS

I Am a Local Tour Guide

"I live in the coolest neighborhood in the world. I think so, anyway. My neighborhood was a planned community built by a railroad company in the early 1900s and is a perfect example of a factory town. It's actually a neighborhood within a very large city, and nobody knows more about it than I do.

I didn't grow up in this neighborhood. I discovered it in college, first by reading about it and then by coming here to see it for myself. The history here is incredible. When this neighborhood was built, the company was one of the largest employers in the city. It built railroad cars for railroads around the country, which was a very big business at the time. The company employed a lot of people and figured it could save everybody money by building a planned community for company employees to live in. They built houses and apartments catering to the various kinds of employees, from small apartments for junior workers to lavish houses for senior executives. They also built community centers, school buildings and even shops. It was revolutionary for its time. The architecture is fascinating, too.

I moved to this neighborhood after college when I got a job nearby. I was thrilled to live in such a great neighborhood and immediately got involved in local organizations. I became an expert on the local history, too. I started giving tours almost by accident. When friends and family came to visit, I took them on informal tours. I soon discovered, however, that my tours were really pretty slick. Everybody enjoyed them, and I received lots of compliments on my extensive local knowledge.

So why not? I whipped up a website and started offering tours on weekends. I didn't charge much, but I didn't have many expenses, either, and I got a lot of tips. After a couple of years, I quit my regular job and established relationships with larger tour companies in the city. Subcontracting has been a real blessing for my little business. The big tour companies offer my tour as part of their larger itineraries. They do essentially all the work and bring me new customers every day. I charge them a little less than I do regular tourists but I get a lot more business.

I've thought about expanding my business to include some other neighborhoods. I've also thought about sending out a few résumés and seeing if I can land a spot as a full-time tour guide for a big company operating around the world. I love my neighborhood but I've also developed a new skill. Maybe it can take me somewhere I haven't been."

I Am an Adventure Tour Guide

"I am a safari director. I set up tents on the plains of Tanzania and show people the wildlife and natural splendors they've only seen in pictures. I'm like Indiana Jones meets the Jungle Cruise. I couldn't be happier.

I came to this job in a very roundabout way. I majored in international relations in college and then joined the military, where I became a foreign area officer, or FAO. My specialty was Africa. I spent many years traveling around the continent, working with local militaries and State Department personnel from US embassies and their counterparts from other countries. I learned several local languages, too. I loved my job, and didn't really want to give it up.

Military personnel can retire with a generous pension after only 20 years of service, so I was still pretty young when I took off my uniform for the last time. I was done with military life but I had no intention of leaving Africa. I found a job as a tour guide with a safari company.

Frankly, I thought I was overqualified for the job. I was wrong. There was a lot to learn. For starters, most regular people don't like to be treated like soldiers. They don't want to live in tents without amenities. They don't want to eat boring food. They certainly don't want to be ordered around by the person they are paying to show them a good time. Customer service did not come easily to me but I figured it out eventually by working alongside a seasoned professional for a couple of years.

I definitely had the logistics down, however. If you want to move 25 people and all of their stuff from Point A to Point B, across the veldt, over a river or two and into an area with no support services, I'm the person to call. The military may not be much at customer service but we're really good at moving stuff around the world.

I love this career because I never get tired of helping other people to appreciate the wonders of Africa. Everybody has seen safari footage on TV but it's entirely different when you see it in real life. I always get a thrill when I see people's eyes open wide the first time they see a lion in the wild or a herd of gazelle bounding across the plains.

The logistics can be very challenging and some customers don't really know what they're getting into. Even with all the support we provide, a safari can be difficult for people accustomed to comfy hotels with all the amenities. Most of them get into it and learn to enjoy themselves. There's nothing I would rather be doing."

I Am a Tour Director

"I am the classic tour director. I take busloads of tourists around Europe for two weeks at a time.

I got into this business when I worked as a tour guide after college. I majored in history and minored in French and figured that a couple of years leading tourists around Europe would be fun. I worked alongside a seasoned tour director and led tours to historic sites and attractions in the cities we visited. I tagged along for the entire tour but was only responsible for my tours, not the overall logistics of the operation.

I've been to the Eiffel Tower a million times but it never fails to impress me. It looks all light and airy in photos but in real life it is huge and imposing. Impressive. I could say the same thing about many of the landmarks of Europe. I never get tired traveling here.

My work can get a little repetitive, however. I may have seen the Eiffel Tower a million times but most of my clients are seeing it for the first time. I always get a little charge out of watching the expressions on their faces when they realize how magnificent it is. I concluded a long time ago that getting into a rut would take all the fun out of this career. I got into the tour business in part to broaden my own horizons. Seeing the same things over and over again wasn't going to help with that.

So I became a tour director. As a director, I have a lot more control over the content of tours. Yes, we still go to the Eiffel Tower but we also go to other places that aren't necessarily on everybody's itinerary, like the beaches of Normandy where American, British and Canadian soldiers landed during World War II. I also tweaked my standard itinerary to spend an extra day in Belgium. Often overlooked by tour operators, Belgium is home to incredible cuisine and should not be missed. I think it's important to shake things up once in a while. If I didn't I would soon drone on like somebody reading from a script.

Clients can sometimes be a handful. While this is true of any customer service job, it is especially true in the tour business because I am always with my clients. Retail sales clerks may have to deal with unhappy customers but those customers walk away after a few minutes. Mine sit next to me on the bus for weeks at a time, and they are in a hotel room right down the hall from mine. That makes customer service extra important. If you want to get into this business because you think traveling all the time will be nothing but fun, you're only half right. If you don't have what it takes to provide excellent customer service you should stick to traveling on your own time. Great customer service is what sets one company apart from the others."

I Own an International Tour Company

"I founded my company nearly 40 years ago. I had just finished a college degree in business administration and had no desire to go straight into the corporate world. So I filled up a backpack, bought a round-trip ticket to Rome and spent a few months wandering.

When I returned home, a few friends asked me if I would be willing to lead them on a tour of some of my favorite places. They didn't pay me for the tour, but I figured out the itinerary and made all the arrangements. Everybody had a great time, so my friends started talking about me to their friends. I was onto something.

Then I took another group on the same tour. They weren't friends, so I treated them like customers and charged them a fee large enough to cover my own expenses and leave me a little profit. It worked, but it was a little awkward. The people on that second tour were customers, not buddies. I needed to be on my best professional behavior at all times. I was there to serve them, not to hang out with them.

I continued doing tours, adding different itineraries and keeping things interesting. Eventually I hired a few guides and directors who could take over my original itineraries while I looked into others. I created itineraries for most of Europe, and then expanded into the Caribbean and Latin America. After a few more years I expanded into Africa and Asia. I never really set out to build a global tour business, but I'm sure glad things worked out the way they did.

PERSONAL QUALIFICATIONS

GOOD TOUR OPERATORS SHARE SOME fundamental qualities. Excellent customer service skills are essential, both for your relations with your clients and with your suppliers. Tour operators are in the business of selling experiences that people want. Customer service is an indelible part of that experience. People on a tour come home with memories and a souvenir or two. As a tour operator, the service you provide will be inseparable from the larger experience. Either you get your clients from the airport to the hotel promptly, then to the restaurant where their tables are waiting, then off to Machu Picchu well rested and on time – or you do fail in any detail. When you are telling a group all about the history of Washington Square in New York City the only things they care about are that you get it right, make it entertaining, suggest a reliable place they can have lunch, and know where the nearest public restrooms are.

Running a tour is a logistical challenge. Imagine you are meeting 20 customers at a hotel in London for a week-long tour of the British capital. For you, that means booking 13 hotel rooms – for couples and a few singles – a motor coach for getting around, theatre tickets for two nights, 21 meals – some at unusual or especially interesting places you have discovered – entrance to two castles and three museums, and 21 Segways – with wireless headsets – for the riverfront tour on Thursday. If it rains on Thursday, you had better have a backup plan for the riverfront tour. If the big-ticket exhibit at one of the museums unexpected closes the day before you are supposed to go there, you are going to need to come up with an alternative. Not just any alternative, but a plan that will make the clients feel like they got lucky! A flair for organization and imagination will be essential.

You will also need a thorough knowledge of your subject. Your clients will know when you are genuinely enthusiastic about your subject, and when you are just reciting from a prepared script. The best tour operators have a passion for their subjects that they can share with their clients.

ATTRACTIVE FEATURES

YOU GET PAID TO DO SOMETHING that most people pay to do! How many times have you been on a tour and thought to yourself, "I could give this tour myself." Tours – and the vacation packages they are wrapped up in – are luxuries that people choose to spend their time and money on. They are interesting, fun and often exciting. Most people are happy to pay to indulge in them, and you are not the first person who has taken a tour and wondered what it would be like to be the tour leader. To live that life, day in and day out, would have to be exciting and fun. Being paid for it is even better. If you have a genuine interest in your subject, there could be nothing better than getting paid to share that knowledge with others.

Most people get into the tour business because they have a strong intellectual fascination with a place or activity. The guides who lead city tours, for example, are almost always huge fans of their city, whether they grew up there or not. They read books on their city in their spare time and never get tired of chatting with tourists about their favorite subject. The same goes for tour operators who specialize in activities. The people who choose to set up a mountain-biking tour business in Alaska are obviously into this activity themselves. The owners and guides of such a business are probably the first to the top of the mountain every time because they love what they do. What fascinates you?

Many tour operators start their own businesses after working for somebody else for a few years. The business also offers endless opportunity for entrepreneurs. Can you think of a new spin to put on an old tour? Various companies use the same neighborhood in Chicago to conduct architecture tours, history tours of Prohibition-era Chicago, and pub crawls to local restaurants and bars, for example. Never assume that one place or activity is overexposed. There is always a new angle just waiting for the right entrepreneur to bring it to life. Barriers to entry are low. To start a simple neighborhood history tour all you really need is an idea, a website, and some comfortable shoes.

UNATTRACTIVE ASPECTS

THE TOUR BUSINESS HAS ITS DRAWBACKS. Because so many people want to work in it, the tour business is very competitive. You are not the only person who thinks it would be cool to offer zip-lining adventures in the Rocky Mountains. Where there are mountains with fantastic scenery and countless trees to attach zip lines to, there will be many companies offering zip-lining adventures. You will have to compete to attract customers, which could mean reducing prices, offering longer tours, tours of beautiful unknown places you have discovered, staying open for a few extra weeks or months every year, or even offering additional services on site, like a café or gift shop to attract additional customers and make more money. Go to a popular tourist destination like Washington, DC and you will see dozens of tour buses lined up in front of every main tourist attraction every day. They all represent different companies and are in constant competition to attract tourists.

Another problem is red tape and restrictions. Many tour companies offer access to places or activities that are heavily regulated by government. Want to offer day cruises to watch the whales off California? You will have to jump through hoops erected by the Environmental Protection Agency, the US Coast Guard, and several state agencies before you can even get started. Until 2015, the city of Savannah, Georgia required all tour guides working in the city to earn a license by passing a comprehensive test. That requirement was dropped after several tour guides filed a lawsuit alleging that the city violated their First Amendment right to free speech, but the issue illustrates the problems with red tape faced by tour operators everywhere. Want to take mountain-bikers on a tour of a national park? The National Park Service will have many restrictions and limitations you will have to abide by.

Any career can become just a job after doing it long enough. You may think that will never happen. How could you ever get tired of leading tourists around the Taj Mahal, but after the thousandth time you tell the story of the emperor's love for his wife who died in childbirth you may realize that the story has lost its charm, and you are just going through the motions. You can always tell bored tour guides. This may happen to you.

EDUCATION AND TRAINING

THE EDUCATION AND TRAINING THAT YOU will need have more to do with what you want to achieve than with any rules or requirements. Most people who pursue this career do so because they are following a dream, but it is also important to be practical and well prepared.

The simplest route to a career in the tour business is to earn a degree in tourism and hospitality. Specialized business degrees, with an emphasis in tourism and hospitality, give students a broad overview of basic business principles like marketing, management, accounting and finance, and add tourism-specific courses in subjects like customer service and event management. Most degrees offer specializations, including restaurant management, hotel management, and broader concentrations like tourism that touch on everything. Many universities offer bachelor's degree programs in tourism and hospitality, and more and more graduate programs are being offered every year.

You can also earn a bachelor's degree in business administration and fine-tune your studies with a few courses in hospitality management and an internship with a business in the hospitality industry.

Many tour operators get into the business because they are driven by enthusiasm for something, usually a place or an activity. Depending upon what motivates you, you could earn a degree in history, philosophy, geography, culinary arts, sociology, art, or languages, for example. A degree in sports management, sports science, physical therapy or recreation would be ideal for careerists who prefer active tours. A number of tour operators started out doing something else and got into the tour business later in life after discovering a passion for a place or activity.

Want to see the world while you are still young? Join the military! Do a five-year hitch and cash in the GI Bill to go to college. You will do some very interesting travel along the way.

There is no better way to gain hands-on experience than by completing an internship during your college years. Simply put, an internship is a job related to your major that takes the place of coursework for a summer or semester. Most internships are paid and many come with special opportunities not available to regular employees, like seminars, behind-the-scenes tours or meetings with senior leaders. Your duties may range from making coffee, to looking over the shoulders of professionals hard at work, to actually contributing to work in progress.

Many careerists get their first real jobs after college with the boss who hired them as interns, which is an added bonus. On the other hand, sometimes the experience gained during an internship is enough to persuade someone to change their major and try something else.

There are other credentials you should seriously consider if you want to get into the tour operations business.

United States Tour Operators Association (USTOA) Specialist credential. Offered by the USTOA Travel Agent Academy, the Specialist program teaches careerists best practices in the travel and tour industry.

The American Society of Travel Agents offers the Tour Operator Program, or TOP.

The International Air Transport Association offers many courses in travel and tourism.

The International Tour Management Institute offers certificates for tour guides and for tour directors.

Learning at least one foreign language will be very helpful to your career. This is important for two reasons: First, tour companies arrange tours around the world and are always in need of guides and directors who speak local languages so they can conduct business effectively. Second, tour operators often offer tours for groups based on the language spoken by their clients. If enough Japanese-speaking tourists sign up for a particular tour, the tour operator would be wise to offer the tour in Japanese, and you could be the guide to do it.

EARNINGS

EARNINGS IN THE TOUR OPERATIONS AND marketing business very widely depending upon the type of job, employer, and whether the job is full time or part time. Many entry-level jobs pay relatively little in the beginning. On the other hand, dedicated entrepreneurs can make millions.

Tour guide is often a careerist's entry into the tour operations and travel marketing business. Tour guide jobs come in all shapes and sizes. Many tour guides are self-employed entrepreneurs who offer tours of interesting places or lead activity tours. Such guides may conduct most or all of their business in cash, sell tickets for each tour, and keep the proceeds as their earnings. Tour guides employed by tour companies may be paid an hourly wage of anywhere from minimum wage to $25 per hour. Tour guides often receive tips after each tour, which can add considerably to their income.

Tour directors manage tour operations. Their

responsibilities typically include hiring and training tour guides and managing the day-to-day business of tours. Tour directors are entry-level managers and can earn anywhere from $35,000 to $75,000 per year. That is a pretty wide range, but some tour companies are relatively small and provide simple services. Others are large, complex and provide services to other companies, like cruise lines. The more sophisticated the business, the larger the paycheck.

If you own the business, the sky is the limit. The tour operations and marketing business offers innumerable opportunities for entrepreneurship. Want to make a few extra dollars in your spare time during college? Start a company to give tours of historic buildings with notable architecture in your city. If you are a little more ambitious you can look into starting something bigger, like buying a boat and offering skyline cruises around the waterfront and local rivers. Want to learn to fly a plane? The skies over Hawaii are filled with small planes carrying tourists on hour-long sightseeing trips around volcanoes and waterfalls. If you are really savvy, you will figure out how to hook up with a larger company like a cruise or bus line and let them sell your tours to their customers.

  Destination marketing managers and senior executives at major tour companies can earn salaries of $100,000 per year or more. These professionals specialize in the touring business and almost always climb the ladder from the bottom. Competition for these top-level jobs is tough. If your goal is to work your way into one of these jobs someday, you had better get moving now!

OPPORTUNITIES

THE TOUR OPERATIONS AND MARKETING industry is thriving more than ever, presenting plenty of opportunity for ambitious careerists. When it comes to spending their touring dollars, consumers are more demanding than ever.

There was a time when a city-a-day bus tour of Europe was just about the most adventurous thing most people wanted to do. There is even a joke about them: "If it's Tuesday, this must be Belgium!" Rich people went on safaris in Kenya and really ambitious tourists went whitewater rafting in the Grand Canyon. All of these tours are still popular today, but they have almost become mundane. Sure, a month-long bus tour of Europe is a good way to see a little of everything, but how about a river cruise through Europe instead? Or a bicycle tour of the French wine country? Or a tour of boutique farms and specialty food producers in southern Italy? Kenyan safaris are still popular, but seeing Victoria Falls on the border between Zambia and Zimbabwe is a truly memorable experience.

Demand for ever-more-exotic tours is driven by the fact that the world is getting smaller every day. Wonders that were once the exclusive province of documentaries can now be seen by everybody all the time on the Internet. Combined with lower airfares and better connections around the world it is only natural that people would say, "I want to go there." About the only phenomenon that can slow down this process is war, terrorism, and other kinds of unrest that make certain parts of the world too dangerous to visit.

Given the combination of wider knowledge and easier access there is always room for one more great idea. Who knew that millions of people would pay real money to zipline down mountains and take in the views? Or to visit empire penguin colonies on the Arctic? There is no limit to human curiosity and no limit to the market for tour operators eager to fulfill it. No matter what your personal fascination, there can be a place for you in this business.

GETTING STARTED

SETTING YOUR SIGHTS ON YOUR FIRST REAL JOB can be an intimidating prospect. This is the time to make yourself known to as many potential employers as possible. First, make sure your résumé and other personal marketing materials are in order. A good résumé is absolutely essential to finding a good job. A résumé is your first impression, and you want it to be a good one. Spell out everything you have ever done that relates in any way to the tour business. As a new job seeker, you should be willing to put everything on the table. You never know what might catch an employer's eye. If you are unsure of your résumé writing skills, there are innumerable books and applications on the market that can help you. Your university's outplacement office may also offer assistance. There are also professionals who will provide their services for a fee. Be sure to create a traditional résumé that can be printed on paper even if most of the jobs you apply for ask you to enter your information into an online form. A ready-made résumé will make it easy to cut and paste information into online forms and will make sure that you do not accidentally change or embellish your information as you go.

Once you have your résumé ready to go, get in touch with everybody you know in the tour operations and marketing business and send it to them. It is very common for new careerists to get their first jobs with the companies where they completed an internship. Teachers and former employers are often happy to give new careerists a helping hand by passing around their résumés or providing references. Even if none of these people can give you a job, you may find that somebody has a friend who knows somebody who recently had lunch with the owner of a tour company who needs somebody just like you. You never know.

Most importantly, keep the faith. You are your own product, so always be sure to make yourself look as good as possible. Be on time, do some research on potential employers before you go to interviews and always be polite. Keep an open mind, too. You may think you know what your dream job would be, but do not let that vision stand in the way of a pretty good job that may teach you something while paying a salary. The most important thing you can do right now is get into the business and start to make a name for yourself. Worry about fine-tuning your career after you have been at it for a few years. Just get out there and give it your best. Good luck!

ASSOCIATIONS, PERIODICALS, WEBSITES

■ **Abercrombie and Kent**
www.abercrombiekent.com

■ **Adventures by Disney**
www.adventuresbydisney.com

■ **Adventure Travel Trade Association**
www.adventuretravel.biz

■ **American Society of Travel Agents**
www.asta.org

■ **Association of Independent Tour Operators**
www.aito.com

■ **Audley**
www.audleytravel.com

■ **Butterfield & Robinson**
www.butterfield.com

■ **Cameroon Travel and Tours**
www.cameroontravelandtours.com

■ **Collette**
www.gocollette.com

■ **Conde Nast Traveler**
www.cntraveler.com

■ **Elder Treks**
www.eldertreks.com

■ **Enchanting Travels**
www.enchantingtravels.com

■ **European Tourism Association**
www.etoa.org

■ **Expedia**
www.expedia.com

■ **Flyer Talk**
www.flyertalk.com

■ **Fodor's Travel**
www.fodors.com

■ **Grand European Travel**
www.getours.com

■ **Hipmunk**
www.hipmunk.com

■ **Holiday Pirates**
www.holidaypirates.com

■ **International Air Transport Association**
www.iata.org

■ **International Tour Management Institute**
www.itmitourtraining.com

■ **Jetsetter**
www.jetsetter.com

■ **Kensington Tours**
www.kensingtontours.com

■ **Lindblad Expeditions**
www.expeditions.com

■ **Lonely Planet**
www.lonelyplanet.com

■ **Luxury Retreats**
www.luxuryretreats.com

■ **Micato Safaris**
www.micato.com

■ **National Tour Association**
www.ntaonline.com

■ **Odysseys Unlimited**
www.odysseys-unlimited.com

■ **Road Scholar**
www.roadscholar.org

■ **Tauck**
www.tauck.com

■ The Crazy Tourist
www.thecrazytourist.com

■ Thomas Cook Group
www.thomascookgroup.com

■ Transitions Abroad
www.transitionsabroad.com

■ Travel Journeys of a Lifetime
ww.traveljourneysofalifetime.com

■ Trip Advisor
www.tripadvisor.com

■ United States Tour Operators Association
www.ustoa.com

■ US Tour Operators Association
www.travelpulse.com

■ Visit Sierra Leone Travel
www.visitsierraleone.org

■ Wildland Adventures
www.wildland.com

Copyright 2018

Institute For Career Research CHICAGO

CAREERS INTERNET DATABASE
www.careers-internet.org